CW00384068

Preface

Preface

In this workbook I'm going to share with you the techniques and mental models I've used every time I'm struggling to quit an addiction.

I am by no means an expert in psychology, behavioral studies, rehabilitation, medicine or any related field of work. What I am is a young man who's used many addictive substances over the years and always gotten rid of them by trying out, evaluating, examining and understanding these key concepts and myself.

I've often thought about why addictions never really became an issue for me. After all, I've been warned about them half my life because they are present in my close family. Since I was a teenager I've used caffeine, nicotine, alcohol and countless different drugs. Because of my predisposition for addiction I have been very careful not to form any addictions right from the beginning. But I still had to satisfy my overwhelming curiosity. This has led me to learn and develop many protective habits and ways to shield my mind from addictions. The ones I'm sharing with you in this book.

Later in my life I fell in love with systemizing things. Realizing that I have an actual system for controlling addictions and seeing how hard it is for so many people, I decided to write this workbook. If you apply these methods, I have no doubt you'll succeed in quitting your addiction.

There are many kinds of addictions. In this workbook we'll go over the ones caused by substance abuse. However, you can use many of the lessons here to treat other kinds of addictions as well but you might have to apply them in a different way than explained here.

Every rule and thought I introduce you to is either my own conclusion or an already well-known concept that I have applied for this purpose. Many of these rules are not just great for this cause, but rather great ideas allround you can apply to anything in life.

The best way I've found to describe addiction to someone who doesn't understand it, is comparing it to waking up. Everyone knows how their brain works when they're going to sleep and promise themselves they'll wake up early for whatever the reason. The next morning when the alarm rings and you wake up an hour earlier than usual, do your thoughts feel like they did last evening? Are you still excited about this? Or are you going over the thought process of "maybe this isn't important", "I think I'll sleep now and try again next week" or "Well I think I need to sleep today because there's this important meeting which I totally forgot to account for yesterday". Recognise this? That's exactly how it feels to try and end an addiction without a plan. Making decisions is easy when you don't actually feel the consequences.

The worst part about this is that it happens so easily, and if you fail to fight it once it may happen again. And we really don't want to make a habit out of this, because giving up is easy and it gets easier the more you do it.

Then how do we counter this? That's exactly what I'm going to share with you.

How to use this workbook

This is a workbook and I assume you didn't get this book to enjoy literature. Good. You will find tasks in this book and the purpose is to get you to think and give you tools to challenge yourself for the better. But, the idea is to make the changes you're looking for as easy as possible, so don't worry about that challenging part too much. That's why there's this how-to part for you.

You can read this workbook just as you wish, but this is the way I'm recommending so you can get as much out of this book as possible. If you're like me, you might find yourself thinking "this is hard, why am I doing this?". But remember, it was you who wanted to solve a problem. This book is only here to make it easier for you. It's a cliche, but remember that no one's gonna come and push you to get through this. It's just you and this workbook.

I recommend you skim through this book first. After that, you'll have an idea of the concept and it's easier to understand what you're getting into. When that's done, you can start reading. There are 10 rules and after each rule you'll find a summary of that rule and an assignment for you to complete, relating to that rule. I suggest you either;

A. Read a rule, read it's summary and then complete the assignment one by one

OR

B. Read all the rules and their summaries first, then go back to the first rule and start working through the rules by reading just the summary and then completing the assignment.

The idea of these assignments is to get you to really understand the rule and how to apply it to your own situation. Without this, there's a risk of this book being just pretty words on your screen.

After each assignment, there is a box where you can write your notes regarding that rule and the assignment. You hate writing? Don't worry I got you! I have dyslexia and ADHD so I get it. I don't like it either. So here's some options for you to use instead of writing the assignments in nice full sentences:

1. Bullet point lists
2. Mind maps
3. Voice recordings
4. Drawing
5. Visualization
6. Whatever works for you.

But I think this is enough for instructions. So, happy reading!

Rule 1: Have your why figured out

Simon Sinek has a famous TED Talk and a book on a topic he calls The Golden Circle. Sinek explains the concept that consists of three important questions: Why, How and What? When you do something you should be able to answer these questions. Why are you doing this? How will you do this? What is it you're trying to achieve?

You already have the What - you're ending an addiction. This workbook will give you the tools, so there's your How. But you'll still need your Why. Why? Because that's what you're telling yourself when you start doubting the process and what's the point of all this. If there's no clear Why, there'll be no success. If something is pointless it at least needs to be fun for us to do it. Giving up an addiction is usually not fun, no matter how easily bearable we make it.

Make your Why something exciting and easily understandable. Something you can see and feel every day. Something you look forward to. Not just overall health, but also better teeth. Not just healthy lungs in the future but also a fresh breath and a better sense of taste. Ideology is nice and we think it's better because it's more meaningful, but that's not what our brain feels. It's often more effective only in theory.

Key takeaways

- You need to have a clear understanding of why you're doing this. This is the whole basis of your motivation and your will to push through.

- Your Why has to be something you're excited about. Something concrete that you are eagerly waiting for. Forget about what you think is the right thing to be excited about and be honest with yourself. You don't have to share your reasons with anyone.

Your assignment

Why, why, why, why, why? That's your first assignment. To really get a good understanding of why you're doing this, we won't just ask why. We'll repeat that question until you are really content with the answer. It usually takes around five Whys.

Let's take an example. Why did you get this workbook? "Because I want to quit smoking" Why do you want to quit smoking? "Because I want to be healthier" Why do you want to be healthier? "Because I want to be able to play with my kids and maybe even grandchildren in the future" and so on.

You repeat this until you're really happy with the answer and it makes sense to you. This way you get multiple different reasons from superficial to deeply meaningful. Write down your answers. If you feel like you want to give up later, refer back to this task and think about your Whys.

Your notes:

Rule 2: Inform your social circle so they can support you

We are social animals by nature. Like it or not, you are most likely affected by the opinions and support or the lack of it you get from others. I strongly suggest you inform the people around you about your goal and have them support your process right from the beginning. The people around us have a huge impact on how we act, that's why it's important to use this as a resource rather than an obstacle.

Let's say smoking is what you're trying to get rid of. Tell the people you usually have a smoke with to not ask you to come at all. It's harder to say no if someone is asking you to join.

Remember that the risk of doing something like this at the same time with someone comes with the risk of one of you quitting. This makes it a lot easier for the other one to relapse. This risk multiplies with the people involved. So consider doing this alone, then recommending this to a colleague or a friend when you've succeeded. But if you really want to do this with someone and feel like it's the better way for you, feel free to do that. You know yourself best.

Key takeaways

- Inform the people around you, so they can support your process. It's best if you communicate directly how you want them to support you. Is it something they shouldn't say, or could they help by not doing something around you?

- If possible, try to go through this process alone so someone else quitting won't affect your process.

Your assignment

Think ahead who you're interacting with most of the time. Then think about what you are going to tell them. What do you want or don't want them to do to support you?

Write down the things you want or don't want people to do or say about your process. Then write down how you want to ask them to support you with this, referring back to what you just wrote down.

Your notes:

Rule 3: Fight emotional triggers with visualization before they happen

Emotional triggers are tough. There's the addiction itself that's making it hard to quit, but when you add some other unrelated mental stress factor in there, it's hard to fight the urges. You feel down and then you start thinking about what would make you feel better. The first thing will always be what you're addicted to.

Then how can we overcome this? The best solution is to work that out beforehand. Go over the situations and your responses in your mind before they happen. Like a boxer training to counter his opponent's punch, you engrain the response in your mind. Our goal is that next time when you have a fight about the dishes with your significant other and would normally go smoke joint to calm down, you'll now find yourself reaching out for a cup of tea instead.

It has been studied that visualization can be nearly as effective as actual practice. You're using the same neural pathways and strengthening them. By imagining the situation that normally causes you to relapse and then the response you want, you're forming a habit you want. Not the habit you're used to.

This is a rule for harder situations and not everyone needs this. But for the stickiest addictions and for more emotional people this is a great way to finally get over the harder moments.

Key takeaways

- If you tend to fail during emotional distress, use visualization to combat relapsing.

- The more you use visualization the better you get and the better the results get.

- Go over the situations you usually relapse in on your head. Visualize yourself responding to that stressful situation in a way you would want to react. Try to immerse yourself with all your senses in that situation. Imagine the feeling after successfully making the better decision and realizing that you finally broke the pattern.

Your assignment

Visualize the most common situation where you relapse: First think through what usually happens, then think how you would want that to go. Visualize the best response to that situation. A response in which you don't relapse. Write down the most important parts of these thoughts, so you can easily go over them again later. Repeat the visualization as often as you need to.

Your notes:

Rule 4: Scale down your daily consumption

Maybe the most simple and effective of all the rules in this workbook. The extremely important concept of scaling down. What's the one thing every doctor will tell you if you're quitting an addictive medicine? Scale down.

Don't try to go cold turkey, no matter how hardcore you want to be. It's not good for your mind, soul or body. What should you do then? You scale down. You take small steps, don't go too fast or too slow. You map out the whole time frame it takes for you to quit, so you have an end date to look forward to. You'll actually know when you will have made it. Now that's a great motivator!

When I say don't go too fast, you might understand right away that this is to avoid the withdrawal symptoms. You can still make progress every day by taking smaller steps.

But why shouldn't you go too slow? Well this is all about your motivation. What you want is to constantly feel like you're making progress. It's so much easier to stay motivated for one month than it is for six months. A month feels like a cool project you're happy to do. Six months is a heavy commitment. And we're not building a Fortune 500 company or training for the Olympics here.

What I recommend for most situations is one month and that's also the default time frame in this workbook.

Key takeaways

- Scale down with small decrements.

- One month is a good rule of thumb.

- Make it so that it's hard to notice a difference between two consecutive days.

- All the instructions for scaling down are at the end of this book right above The Four Week Plan -table.

Your assignment

Think of the best way to scale down in one month, going from your daily portion to zero. Let's say you want to stop using caffeine. You're now drinking 5 cups a day. Going from 5 to 4 should be relatively easy, but how will you transition between 2 and 1? How about 1 to zero? A hint: half cups, more milk, different coffee, different caffeine drink with less caffeine. Write down all the guidelines and tips for you to use later when you get to the end of this book.

Your notes:

Rule 5: Replace the habit with something similar

What you're addicted to is usually not the only part you're craving. It's the habit itself. Luckily that's quite easy to fix. You can either find a way to replace it right away, or then change the form of the substance first and then replace that.

You can also work this in with the scaling down. For example changing between normal and decaf coffee, or whatever you're working with.

Habits can be especially hard if they have some benefits or positive factors. For example it's a different thing to just stop eating nicotine gum or change to a normal gum than it is to give up the nice little cigarette breaks outside with your friends. This is why it is easier in some situations to first change the form you're getting the addictive substance in, so you can first get used to that and then later on end it easier with these methods.

Note that if quitting the habit itself is not difficult for you, you don't have to make use of this rule just for the sake of it.

Key takeaways

- Change the substance to a similar habit slowly, while you are progressing. This way you can still enjoy the habit.

- If, however, the substance you're addicted to is in a form that is hard to replace, change it to something that is easier to replace beforehand.

Your assignment

Think over the options you have. What form of the substance you use would be the easiest to replace? Write down all forms you know of. For example, cigarettes, nicotine gum, nicotine patches etc. Then think about which of those would be the easiest to use and then replace. Now you have a list you can choose from, if it's necessary or helpful in your situation.

Your notes:

Rule 6: Take care of physical withdrawal symptoms

Physical withdrawal symptoms are just signs that you're going in the right direction. As said earlier, the goal of our tapering off approach is to avoid any problems with withdrawal effects. But of course it is possible to still get some symptoms. Normally the best approach is to treat the cause of the symptoms itself, but when you're ending an addiction it's obviously not possible.

The best way to address any symptoms that might arise is to make yourself comfortable and cut yourself some slack. Having a headache? Drink some water and take it easy. Don't stress it if you're a bit behind with the laundry. How long have you been addicted? Is one month too long of a time compared to it? I doubt it. I would guess you've used more time with the addiction than there is in one month and used more money on it than you can make in a month.

Try to avoid forming any new addictions when you're making yourself feel better. Don't replace sugar with coffee or alcohol with cigarettes.

If the symptoms are interfering with everyday life and you can't ignore them anymore, you can adjust the end date accordingly. Just don't go higher with the dose, but stay with what you're now going with for a little longer.

Key takeaways

- If you get overwhelming withdrawal symptoms, adjust the end date and stay with the dose you're now going with.

- Those symptoms are a sign you're going in the right direction.

- Take care of the symptoms by making yourself comfortable any way you can. Just avoid forming new addictions.

Your assignment

Think of five different ways you can make yourself comfortable if you get withdrawal symptoms. Make sure you don't cause any new addictions. Write them down and refer back to them if you get any symptoms.

Also, think beforehand how you are going to modify your schedule if you need to do that at some point, write it down and stick to it.

Your notes:

Rule 7: Control your surroundings

Ever heard that study where kids ate marshmallows and they then predicted those kids' future success?

I'm talking about the Stanford Marshmallow experiment. If you haven't heard of it, it's a study where they set out to find the correlation between the ability to delay gratification and future success. The key takeaway from that study for us is that our surroundings play a huge factor in our ability to control urges and impulses. Not eating a marshmallow is a lot easier when you don't have any, compared to a situation where there's a bag right in front of you. So control your surroundings and don't tire yourself by having easy access to what you want to give up. There's no point doing that. Your chances of success go way up when you don't make relapse easy for yourself. Getting away without a scratch is easy if you just don't fight when you don't need to.

How can we make it easier when you're tapering off of something? Easiest way to do this is to divide everything into daily portions for the whole month. You know, like meal prepping but for your vices.

If you want, you can then take the daily portions somewhere where it takes a little effort to get them and you don't see them all the time. Any extra you may have? Toss it.

Key takeaways

- Divide your doses into daily portions, only keep portions for a day or a few within reach.

- Hide anything that might cause an impulse to relapse. If you want to stop smoking cigarettes, you should also hide your lighter.

Your assignment

Think of a place where you're going to store your portions for the whole month and then another place that's a bit easier to reach where you can store doses for the next few days. Both of these should be out of sight. The other one might be the attic for example. The other one could be a certain closet or a drawer. Write down all the possible places and pick the two places for you to use.

Your notes:

Rule 8: Stay active or get active

What's just as bad or even worse of a trigger for relapse than negative emotions? No emotions, boredom. When we are bored we naturally start looking for some kind of stimulation. What's the easiest stimulation that comes to mind and you're used to? Your favorite addictive substance.

To avoid those dull moments where your mind starts to wonder back into old habits, you're looking to either get or stay active. Do you have any hobbies? If not, then now is the perfect time to start one. You don't need to get too competitive. The idea is to have fun, enter the flow and consume as much time with activities as possible for the month. Keep your mind occupied but don't stress yourself. This might be harder if you're really competitive by nature, but we have another purpose this time. After this month you can go as hard as you want but for now don't stress about it and have fun.

Staying active can mean going out, playing sports or just occupying your mind with Netflix. The important thing is that it's something you enjoy.

Key takeaways

- Stay active to occupy your mind.

- Have fun any way possible to satisfy your mind without the addiction.

Your assignment

Think of four activities you like to do. One you can do alone at home. One you can do with someone at home. One you can go do alone if you want to get out of the house and one you can do with someone if you want to go out. Write all these down. Some of these might be something you already enjoy and some might be something you've been wanting to try out. You can write more than these four, but write at least one of each.

Your notes:

Rule 9: Don't fight your urges, forget about them all together by distracting yourself

Something important to understand about our thoughts and beliefs is that we can't make them disappear. The neural pathway is there. What we can do however is make a contradicting belief and focus on that. The old one will eventually get weaker. This is why it isn't smart to try to convince yourself to not smoke, but rather to live healthy. Don't focus on not drinking coffee, instead remember to drink something that doesn't have caffeine but you still enjoy.

Don't focus on fighting an addiction. Focus on everything else that doesn't include your addiction and just let it slide away from your life. Or if I were to rephrase this according to what I just said: Focus on your goal. Focus on the addiction free life you're going for. Imagine yourself enjoying life after this one month. See what I did here? In the latter statement I asked you to do something, instead of not doing something. This is what I want you to do when you're thinking to yourself.

Don't give any attention to habits you don't want to hold onto. Give lots of attention to contradicting habits you want to replace the bad ones with and let your unconscious mind do the rest.

Let's take an example. Maybe you drive a car? What do they teach you at a driving school about driving to a curve? You never look at the curve you're driving to, instead you look far ahead where you're going. The car follows your eyes. You cannot drive in the right direction, if you're not looking there. Right?

Key takeaways

- Focus on what you want to achieve and how you will achieve that.

- Avoid thinking about the addiction itself.

Your assignment

Let's do a thought experiment. If you were to repeat yourself the words "Don't drink coffee" a thousand times over the course of 3 days, what drinks or habits would you be thinking about? What if you instead did the same thing with the phrase "Drink hot chocolate". What would probably be on your mind then?

The assignment is this. Think about a habit you might replace your unwanted addiction with. Something as contradicting as possible. Write it down and think about it every time you start thinking about your addiction.

Your notes:

Rule 10: Understand and avoid the dangers association brings

We already went over emotional triggers and boredom. But these are not the only types of triggers there are. The difference between emotional triggers and triggers coming from the outside is how hard they are to control and avoid. This is tied to the concept of controlling your surroundings. To have the best chance of succeeding, you must clean your environment and be mindful of things that you associate with your addiction.

Let's take for example music. Music in particular has been studied in this context by Dr. Genevieve Dingle. Music is great. It's a beautiful thing that can often help us clarify our thoughts and make us feel. The danger lies within the music you associate with the substance. Maybe you've always listened to Pink Floyd while high? Maybe there's some album you like to listen to after a few glasses of wine?

Now what happens when you listen to that same music in some other situation? You automatically start thinking about the associated substance. Most likely it's a craving, but it might be a negative emotion as well. Either way, it's taking you back to what you are trying to leave behind.

I'm not saying you shouldn't listen to your favorite artists ever again. But this is something to be aware of. Remember that this not only applies to music. It might be a certain food, place, person, weekday or anything really. And you can't avoid everything, so be mindful of the dangers of association. If you can't avoid something, at least you can be prepared.

Key takeaways

- Be mindful of the dangers association can bring.

- If it's possible, avoid those dangers at least in the beginning of your process.

Your assignment

Write down everything you personally associate with your addiction. Think through everything that comes to mind. When do you most often experience, see, feel, hear, smell or taste these things? Write them down. Now you have a list to be aware of.

Your notes:

Pulling it all together and last words

If someone could just wipe out an addiction there would already be a service for that. But that's not possible so we're just gonna have to put in the work. Lucky for us, there's always ways to make things easier. This workbook contains many of the ways to help control and end your addictions. I'm confident that you now have the tools to do just that. And you know what they say, "If there's a will, there's a way". You found the way and I assume you already had the will because you found this little guide.

One month is what it takes. But it doesn't have to end there. If you find yourself in a similar situation in the future, you now know what to do. You can go faster or you can go slower. You do you, because you know yourself best. And as I said, not all addictions are bad. I have found what works for me and I have been able to try out different things because of these principles.

In the beginning of chapter nine I talked about having two contradicting beliefs in our head. This causes what's known as cognitive dissonance. That's a fancy psychological term for this phenomenon. Here's why I wanted to come back to this concept:

When cognitive dissonance emerges, you know you're going in the right direction. Just stay with the belief you want to embody. Often when I feel really stressed out and think back about the last few weeks or months, I notice that there's been some big positive changes that I've worked towards for a long time. It's hard going through change, and it often feels the worst during the final moments when you've almost made it through. But that's exactly the moment when you're almost there and should just keep going. The discomfort of change is often for a big part just your mind fighting contradicting beliefs and trying to hold on to a part of itself. Of course part of the discomfort comes from the fact that it is tiring to navigate new habits and beliefs. Just like when you're in a new area, you're constantly aware of your surroundings. If you've been to a new city, you probably know what I mean. For the first few days you feel a little tired, don't you? So don't stop, it's getting easier.

The Four Week Plan

How to plan your four week plan:

1. You can decide the start date as you wish. Either go by your normal workweek or then start whatever day you want and go four weeks from that point on.

2. Read the book through before you start, so you have all the necessary information for the coming weeks.

3. You can either mark this in your own calendar or just draw it on a paper and use that if you don't normally use a calendar.

4. Mark the daily portions you have planned. You get the starting point by estimating your daily consumption at the moment. Your first day should be just a bit under your normal daily consumption. You should get to zero by the end of these four weeks.

5. I suggest you try to get to the smallest possible amount by the end of week three and spend week four using that amount every other day.

6. As an example, let's say you want to give up caffeine. At the moment you drink 5 cups a day. If the smallest

amount that makes any sense to you is half a cup, then that's where you should be at the end of week three. So we have 21 days to go from 5 cups to half a cup. We might go 4 cups, 3 cups, 2.5 cups, 2 cups, 1.5 cups, 1 cup, half a cup.

Here's an example:

I prefer to drop the daily portion faster in the beginning

	Sunday	Monday	Tuesday	Wednesday	Thursday	Friday	Saturday
1st Week	4 cups	4 cups	3 cups	3 cups	3 cups	2.5 cups	2.5 cups
2nd Week	2.5 cups	2 cups	2 cups	2 cups	1.5 cups	1.5 cups	1.5 cups
3rd Week	1 cup	1 cup	1 cup	1 cup	1/2 cup	1/2 cup	1/2 cup
4th Week	No coffee	1/2 cup	No coffee	1/2 cup	No coffee	No coffee	1/2 cup

Here we have a bit longer break before the last day to make the transition easier

Medical and health disclaimer

The publisher and the author are providing this book and its contents on an "as is" basis and make no representations or warranties of any kind with respect to this book or its contents. The publisher and the author disclaim all such representations and warranties, including but not limited to warranties of healthcare for a particular purpose. In addition, the publisher and the author assume no responsibility for errors, inaccuracies, omissions, or any other inconsistencies herein. The publisher and the author are not liable for risks or issues associated with using or acting upon the information on this book or any related material.

This book does not support, advise or encourage drug use in any way. The content of this book is purely for informational purposes, based on the author's personal views.

The content of this book is for informational purposes only and is not intended to diagnose, treat, cure, or prevent any condition or disease and it does not substitute for professional medical advice. You understand that this book is not intended as a substitute for consultation with a licensed practitioner. We advise you to consult a medical professional or healthcare provider if you're seeking medical advice, diagnoses, or treatment. Please consult with your own physician or healthcare specialist regarding the suggestions and recommendations made in this book. The use of this book implies your acceptance of this disclaimer.

The publisher and the author make no guarantees concerning the level of success you may experience by following the advice and strategies contained in this book, and you accept the risk that results will differ for each individual. The examples provided in this book show results, which may not apply to the average reader, and are not intended to represent or guarantee that you will achieve the same or similar results.

Printed in Great Britain
by Amazon

40687146R00030